Minerals: The Rainbow Connection

Nansih Spirit Song

AuthorHouse™
1663 Liberty Drive
Bloomington, IN 47403
www.authorhouse.com
Phone: 1-800-839-8640

First published by AuthorHouse 8/5/2009

ISBN: 978-1-4490-0042-4 (e)
ISBN: 978-1-4490-0041-7 (sc)

Library of Congress Control Number: 2009906279

Printed in the United States of America
Bloomington, Indiana

This book is printed on acid-free paper.

Cover:
© All rights reserved
Nansih Spirit Song
Wildwood Refuge, Grapeland,
Houston County, Texas 75844

Dedication

This treatise is dedicated to the inhabitants of nature's world—sentient or otherwise. They bring me joy and learning. May it always continue.

Sunshine, the smartest dog I've ever known, and Shadow Gordon Setter are still with me in spirit—always my "guard" companions.

Thanks to Chief Speed for the lovely foreword. "Wado" (Cherokee for "Thank you!")

Thanks also to Beth Kerbey for typing the manuscript.

Contents

Foreword

December 2, 2008

I take great pride and feel very honored to be able to write a few words of praise about a very dear and helpful person, Nansih, I have been blessed to know for 20-plus years. I have learned many things about life and cures. I have received many words of wisdom and information, much in the area of healing, and comfort from materials and stones such as crystal, which, when cared for properly, bring healing to the natural body/mind and warmth to our surroundings.

I am a full-blooded Native American, one-half Cherokee and one-half Apache. I was raised with teachings and Native American traditions. I cannot remember any time when we never had crystals in our lodges. I am 72 years young, still without arthritis and many other aches and pains that many people suffer from. I was taught by the Cherokee as well as the Apache medicine men and women. My Cherokee grandmother and my Cherokee mother were medicine women. Our family depended on and stayed healthy on roots, herbs, and stones. My Cherokee great-grandfather George lived to the ripe old age of 100. My great-grandfather of the Apache Nation was Geronimo, the Apache chief with blue eyes like sky. His wife, my great-grandmother, was named Marianetta. She was an honorable woman, something kind of nice. Both sets of great-grandparents' names began with the initials G and M—George, age 113; Geronimo, age 91; Merllie, age 80; Marianetta, age 87.

Bullmoose

Introduction

The rock you are drawn to is the rock for you. It will protect and help with focus during meditation. Don't ever doubt the power of our earth. Every natural thing you see is created by a supreme being. Allow the loveliness to awaken your spirit. The brain cells of Mother Earth (rocks) will help you to enter and walk the beauty way.

Phantom crystals are not mentioned in the general contents of this wee book, but I love working with them. The colors and shapes within the crystal are awesome—a rarity, to say the least. Experiment and be patient. Answers will come.

Don't laugh at some of the suggestions I make. Remember, only the uneducated laugh at things they don't know or understand. In your search for truth, I wish you sapphire skies, a circle of light, golden moonbeams, starlit nights, breathtaking rainbows, and swifts in flight.

Legend

Perhaps it is the vibrational tugging of my ancestral Native American strings, but I felt it appropriate to begin this treatise on the mineral kingdom by explaining "the old way."

The Native American remembers a time when people lived in harmony with all of nature and themselves. It was the "old way," when there was no right or wrong, but simply "the way." People hunted for food, not pleasure. They spoke the language of animals, plants, and each other, and offered prayers of thanks and gratitude for all that nature provided. But then people became greedy. They killed game and each other for sport rather than need. They took from the land more than they could use. They forgot the language of the flowers, bees, and animals. They forgot to give prayers of thanks.

So, the Bear Tribe declared that something must be done. To shoot back might mean the life of one of them. The Deer Tribe suggested that each one bring illness into the world. "Humans out of balance will get sick." It was agreed this was the way to handle the situation. The Plant Tribe felt sorry for the humans and said, "They would offer a cure for every illness, if the human decided to return to the "old way."

Tobacco became the sacred herb. Offered in prayer and ceremony, it would help return humans to the "sacred way" of old. But, if used for pleasure, it would cause cancer—the worst disease.

The Mineral Tribe and Rock Tribe declared that each mineral would have special powers and special vibrations. Quartz Crystal, the chief of the Mineral Tribe, said, "I will be the sacred mineral." I will be used to bring clarity, harmony, balance, and wisdom.

This Cherokee legend may be considered myth to the white man, but it is believed and told (in slightly varying versions) by all the Native American tribes still in existence. One man's myth is another man's religion.

One thing is for certain: The mineral kingdom is the oldest kingdom on Mother Earth, and in our universe and all others. To be "tuned" into the various kingdoms (or tribes) is to allow yourself the privilege of walking in balance, in harmony, and opening the "window" to a higher plane of wisdom and enlightenment.

Twentieth century life bombards the body and spirit to the breaking point, and we no longer walk in balance. But, when you begin to view Mother Earth as alive, and all the elements—winds, rivers, rocks, and nature—as a part of each of us (and as important), then you are on the right road to improving your physical and emotional condition, as well as the physical and spiritual condition of the universe.

All matter is made up of crystals of one form or another. Even water is liquid crystal. There would be no physical form (as we know it) without minerals. The closer crystal formations lie to the magnetic core of the earth, the greater their "strength," or magnetic field. Arkansas is close to the core; therefore, the crystals found there are supercharged with energy. However, all minerals have merit and energy.

Deposits of metals and gemstones abound in the earth. It is Mother Earth's energy field—a unified electromagnetic field of life. Electrical voltage applied to a quartz crystal will produce movement. Mechanical pressure on a crystal will produce voltage. The Curies were studying this phenomenon in the 1800s when they discovered radium.

Shamans used (and continue to use) crystals as healing tools and in ceremonies. Rare crystal arrowheads are sometimes found in fields where Indian encampments occurred, and the use of crystals as a talisman was widespread. Edgar Cayce said that the misuse of crystal power led to the downfall of Atlantis.

What ancient civilizations have always known is being rediscovered by the New Age personalities, individuals that wish to tune into a higher spiritual level. It is a return to the "old way" and, it is hoped, a renewed dedication to the cleansing and protection of ourselves and our environment—our Earth Mother.

It has taken a great deal of time to get into the "mess" we are in. It's going to take a great deal of time for us to get out of it. There are no overnight miracles, but instead there is subtle change. When you align your flow of energy, your inner strength, power, and energy are increased.

There is a life force in all matter. Thoughts have energy; energy has form. So, remember to be careful with your thoughts. Remember to make them positive rather than negative. We create our own reality—our own heaven or hell, depending on our early childhood programming to a great extent. When we were children, our beliefs and what we bring with us (on a spiritual level) into this earth world are held onto in adult life.

Unfortunately, our subconscious is accustomed to negativity gleaned from a world gone negative. It understands it, hangs onto it, and refuses to let go without a struggle. Negativity is so comfortable—so familiar.

Our "chakras," or sensitive centers in our bodies, become blocked, causing disharmony and/or glandular problems. Crystalline deposits form. Your electromagnetic field with life-giving current running throughout becomes short-circuited.

Remember that the body has 60 trillion cells and that a new cell is formed every two or three minutes. The oldest cell would be about five months old. Each cell is alive and aware of all thought, good or bad. So, you've got to get the message to the subconscious and to the body cells. They control healing and your immune system.

If you feel you are under someone's control, you will be. If you feel you are a victim of circumstances beyond your control, you will be. If you feel alone and alienated, you will be. You must learn to take responsibility for your own life. Change is not easy, but practice does make perfect.

Create a positive mental picture, and it becomes a mental reality. Visualize yourself as healthy and happy. Love and accept yourself as you are. You may even look in the mirror each morning and say, "I love and accept you as you are."

Make sweeping motions around your "aura." Brush those negative thoughts away. It is a great start, and don't forget to start each day and finish each night with a prayer of thanks for your gift of life. Run your hand through the air. You have created a circuit of energy. Energy vibrates and you can direct your own energy. Remember that you are an electromagnetic field with current running throughout.

The brain (the master computer) vibrates with varying frequencies, and this is where minerals come into use.

Crystals are living things. Each one is individual and unique, as we are.

Kirlian photography records their energy form. Remember the power of uranium.

The atomic arrangement of quartz crystal is quite similar to the DNA structure of the human body. I (and others) believe that quartz crystal can calibrate the body's rate of vibration.

The six sides of quartz represent the six chakras. The end point is the seventh or crown chakra. Only one percent of crystals mined are double terminated. They both gather and dispense energy.

Quartz generates a flow of electricity, amplifying your current and your positive or inspirational thoughts. They are a marvelous focusing device, what I call "a second attention."

There are many books on the use of minerals that state that you must or must not do this, that, or the other. Each individual is unique and different. Each rock is different and unique. Let your instinct be your guide. There is no right or wrong way. Do whatever is comfortable for you. Pick out your own color stone, your own shape, and use it your way. Don't limit yourself. Don't limit the mineral—be intuitive. The mineral that is meant for you will come to you; even small ones are powerful.

There are right-handed, left-handed, fast-working, slow-working, masculine, and feminine crystals—so what! I stress that you are the master of your own life. Listen to your inner voices.

I wouldn't meditate without my quartz crystal, which was given to me by Wiley. I also sleep with a crystal under my pillow, since mental resistance is less in a sleep state.

One of my cats, "Dumbo Dee," adores crystals and likes to curl up by a large quartz cluster while purring like a well-tuned engine. I have had great success in utilizing crystals as well as color therapy for animal problems—so much so that the next printing of my pet care book will contain a chapter on mineral therapy.

Sun water containing a crystal is beneficial to plants, animals, and humans. I give my minerals a sunbath once in a while, as well as a moon bath, and a rinsing under cool water. That's simply my way.

Knowledge is brought forth, not fed in, and minerals do contribute to our well-being. They are Mother Earth's perfect example of beauty and form, proving that perfection is possible.

Quartz producing its electronic charge now runs computers (memory chips), lasers, VCRs, watches, etc. Ultra sound devices and optical lenses for astronomy are quartz. Quartz filters out ultraviolet rays.

Marcel Vogel, retired IBM scientist, did experiments on purification of water and the aging of wine in seconds with a supercharged crystal. The University of Arkansas is doing extensive tests with crystal and the immune system. This is just the beginning.

With the help of the mind, you can release your body to heal itself. When you isolate your true and inner creative feelings, you are throwing your emotional and physical being out of alignment.

Meditation with crystals (and color) produces a healthier and more peaceful individual. When you know who you are, you will know why you are here, and your spiritual awareness will be elevated.

Lightly tap your thymus gland 14 or 15 times when you think of it. This opens your heart chakra. The thymus gland shrinks with age, and the heart chakra is the key to healing. Stroke, smudge, and cleanse. Your mind is unlimited.

Tap into the flow of energy from Mother Earth. Return to the "old way," and walk the sacred pathway in balance. The mineral tribe will assist you.

The Jewel Connection

My dawn is a sea of carnelian and rose quartz that forms a backdrop for the sapphire skies and citrine sun that follow.

Emerald green grass plays host to myriad diamond dewdrop webs centered by jet-black spiders.

Petrified wood trees with jade green leaves dot the landscape, and riverlets of clear quartz bubble merrily along banks of mottled jasper and moss agate.

Ruby, aquamarine, and brown jasper birds serenade as fluorite, ivory, and tiger-eye butterflies dance to the tune of the nodding topaz, opal, spinel, and golden beryl wildflowers.

At day's end, the citrine sun sends out rays of garnet and fire agate before being enveloped by the lapis lazuli evening sky.

A moonstone moon now rises against a black tourmaline night. Pearl and zircon stars twinkle, while amethyst lilac and ivory gardenia-scented breezes drift gently by.

Magnetite whippoorwills close the obsidian curtain as another gem-studded day draws to a close.

The jewels and treasure of my Earth Mother. Her wonders to behold.   *Nansih*

Rocks

You can imagine a crystal in any form or color you desire. But perhaps you wish to explore the attributes of other rock forms. They all have merit.

Petrified wood. Many colors of petrified wood, all unique, are found in the state of Texas. A veterinarian friend who had two clinics in Dallas used several rocks in his practice. Petrified wood was a favorite. He would take a clean rock, put it in a bowl of distilled water, let it sit for 24 hours, and then allow the sick animal to drink only that water. Of course, the rock had to be large enough so the animal couldn't swallow it. Petrified rock has a marvelous grounding effect on the whole system.

Jasper. Jasper is a rock that comes in many colors, thus providing a multitalented stone. Jasper is supposed to aid in memory, giving psychic abilities a boost. Those who suffer from depression should try carrying a piece of jasper. Breathing problems also improve when jasper is used. It is also a pretty stone.

Amethyst. Amethyst, one of my favorites, is the purple flame of purity and protection. It calms nerves and anxiety. In medieval times, wine glasses were carved from amethyst. It was believed to protect from poisons and overdrinking.

Turquoise. My people call turquoise the "sky" stone because of its color. It teaches us to "walk our talk" and protects the traveler along the way to balance and beauty.

I have listed only four rocks. You may want to check out tourmaline, citrine, lapis, lazuli, and topaz. Investigate and experiment.

Dumbo Dee, The Crystal Cat

Dumbo Dee was Grey Lady's son. She had sons Grey Boy and Tiger, daughter Foxie, then daughters Julie, B.B., and sons Kizmet, and Dumbo.

Dumbo had enormous paws and huge eyes, silky grey and white hair, and the imprint of perfect grey lips, like gray lipstick liner. Dumbo was similar to a Maine Coon cat. He was unique and large, a sweetheart by nature. He also loved rocks in any form and color; he even slept with a few under his bedtime pillow. The only fight he ever had was with Kismet, his brother. Kismet had slammed a favorite rock into the refrigerator front. Dumbo jumped him and around they went. I assured Dumbo that Superglue would mend it.

I wish I had a photo of Dumbo lying across my 18-pound crystal slab purring away and kneading his paws—quite a spirit. I asked him once what he was thinking. He telegraphed his answer, "Nothing," with his enormous eyes.

Dumbo Dee, The Crystal Cat

Momma Grey Lady

Kismet

(Kismet and Dumbo)

Color Breathing

Color is another form of wavelength. Different forms produce TV, radar, laser beam, telephone, etc. We take all these for granted without even a thought. Our forefathers would have scoffed at the idea of laser surgery, television, and space travel. So, remember to keep your mind ever ready for new ideas. You owe it to yourself. No negative thoughts are in this book.

Color breathing presents a blueprint for better health in all life forms, animal or plant. Your positive mental visualization or various healing colors do the work; and thought transference, keen concentration, plus a "stick-to-it," "don't give up" attitude produces excellent results. You must be consistent. Do it daily and results will come. Remember, you didn't learn to walk overnight or ride a bicycle in one afternoon. If at first you don't see any positive results, don't give up, but be persistent and patient. Sometimes it takes months. You will be rewarded.

If I am overly tired and have trouble sleeping, I visualize the ocean washing over me in soothing waves. The green waves ripple over my body with healing color as they come into the shore where I am. As they recede, they flow from my body in an indigo shade pulling away all traces of poisons and fatigue. I visualize this. In moments, I am asleep, and I awaken the next morning fully rested.

When I work with an animal, I first surround her with the rose pink color of love thoughts. Then I imagine my right hand holding a purple light like a spotlight. With this, I go over the body starting at the head, holding my hand about nine inches above the skin. I mentally beam the light slowly over each organ and see it as pure, clean, and healthy. Sometimes an animal may become restless. I concentrate "pink" until she calms down. Sometimes the skin may become warm to the touch. This shows success in treatment. I have found at the end of treatment the animal will be breathing quietly in restful sleep.

Should a color I did not choose come into focus, I go with it. This is guidance from a higher spirit.

Friends have had similar experiences, so don't fight it. If you can't locate a color at first, visualize a rainbow. It's a glorious way to start. Amethyst works well as a purple flame.

Color Therapy— An Extension of Color Breathing

The aura is an electromagnetic field that surrounds everything that is alive. One of its functions is to absorb the white light energy from the atmosphere and change it into color energies that vitalize the different parts of the body.

Surrounding yourself mentally with your inspirational color is like having your own private key to your higher self. A favorite color may not be "the" color either, for psychological studies have shown that people who prefer bold colors tend to gravitate to a person wearing subdued shades or to a room painted in "quiet" colors. The same holds true for persons preferring soft shades—only in reverse.

White has always been thought to be the color for everything, for it contains all colors. Hospitals are white. Uniforms are white. But for some, it is too stark, therefore, repelling. It is still a protective shade and will probably always be associated with spiritual healing and Jesus Christ.

Color therapy is but only one form of healing. And, although it is known worldwide and used with great success, it is still banned in this country by the medical monopoly interested, for the most part, only in drug therapy and surgery.

The medical monopoly folks haven't yet learned to control our minds although they are working on it. So, for now, what we do in our own homes and in our own time is our business. And animals, as well as all life forms, respond beautifully to color. The secret is raising the vibration of an organ or a gland from a lower to a higher and healthier vibration. Color has vibration, as do rocks!

Ask for divine guidance and it will be given. Perhaps a color will come to you in a dream or in a thought. If you are sincere, it will materialize.

When I awaken in the morning, I visualize a spotlight of color beaming downward, creating a pyramid of healing light that surrounds the bed. I repeat the procedure each night before I go to sleep, and I never forget to give thanks. Color breathing will not work as well if there is not faith or a desire for spiritual growth. No negative thoughts are allowed. Remember that?

With practice, anyone can discern the various colors involved. Place a light in front of a light-colored wall, and place a plant, a pet, or a friend in front of both. By concentrating on a focal point, not the whole, you will begin to see the aura "glow." Practice makes perfect.

Solar energy is a healing force, and it is the source for light on which all life depends. Use a stone in the color you wish or visualize.

There are seven major force fields, chakras, in humans and animals alike. These centers attract the following rays:

Red—the lowest center at the base of the spine. Red promotes heat and circulation. Red is indicated in disorders of the blood, anemia, fear, and depression.

Orange—lower back, the spleen, kidneys, chest troubles, gallstones. Both red and orange are powerful colors and should be used with care—often with a subdued shade.

Yellow—middle of the back, solar plexus center, a purifier to the whole system, especially the skin. The digestive system, liver, and intestines (constipation, diarrhea) are toned up by this color. It is the sun color.

Green—the color of nature, of peace, of harmony. It is in line with the heart of spring. The physical heart and blood pressure respond to green. Green is harmony and balance, therefore useful in the disharmony accorded by malignant cancer cells. It tunes up the body.

Blue—at the throat center, the base of the skull. Blue is cooling and astringent.

Inflammations of the throat and fevers are treated with blue. Colic, cuts, and burns respond well to blue ray treatment.

Indigo—the brow center, the forehead, the pineal gland. It clears the psychic currents of the body and aids in the treatment of the eyes, ears, nose, and lungs. Cataracts are to be treated with indigo-charged water.

Violet—the highest vibration of all the cosmic energy rays. It controls the pituitary center and the top of the head. It is useful for all healing, especially mental disorders, concussion, and nerves.

In color breathing, I often visualize the first three colors—red, orange, yellow—flowing upward to the solar plexus of the animal I am working with. I then breathe the last three—blue, indigo, violet—downward from the air. The green ray I visualize as flowing freely through the animal on a horizontal line, seeing the animal as restored to health and well-being. The animal does not have to be present for this to take place. Concentration and a sincere desire to aid is all that is needed. Once again, meditation and a selfless wish to help are essential for success.

Always ask for divine guidance and always remember to give thanks. Life is a gift, a blessing; and to receive knowledge and direction, we must remove all petty and mundane thoughts from our minds and souls. A vessel must be emptied before it can be filled. Remember, no negative thoughts are allowed.

For therapeutic colored water, I take a sterile jar, paint it on the outside with the color desired, and when the paint is dry, I fill it with distilled water, often, with Dr. Willard's water, and set it on the ground, our magnetic field, and in the sun for a couple of hours. Then I give the water to the animal that needs that particular color. The animal doesn't get any other water—only the colored sun water.

For cataracts in animals, I would use indigo sun water. The eyes would be bathed in this pure water twice a day until improvement occurs.

There are color screens available for use in color therapy, but why buy when it is so easy to make what is needed? I go to the local discount store and purchase a pad of colored paper. A piece of this paper placed over the front of a flashlight works just as well as the expensive devices. I have even used white paper colored with either crayons or acrylic pencils to get a desired shade.

Ancient manuscripts show us that in China, India, Egypt, and Tibet, there was a complete knowledge of the art of healing by color science. It is called *Chromotherapy*, and it forms a link from our physical bodies to a higher level of consciousness and awareness—a spiritual awareness.

Disharmony of an organ disrupts the rhythm of the body and disease occurs. The mind can cure, if it is quiet and still and channeled properly. That has been proven by many famous personages. How sad we use less than one percent of our mental capabilities. What wonders we could accomplish!

When I am using color treatment with an animal, I also use foods of the particular shade being worked.

Red foods would mean the use of meat, beets, cherries, red-skinned fruits, and cabbage. *Yellow foods* would mean carrots, egg yolks, apricots, squash, melons, and so on. This should give you a general idea of how it is done.

So, again, patience and persistence are necessary. Good health for our beloved animals could depend on that glorious "rainbow" of color. You are limited only by the limits of your mind. Don't allow yourself to be fenced in. Rocks are great tools for color therapy—the true rainbow connection.

Be strong in faith and your ability to survive the moment of now. The reality of the present is our moment in the sun. You can overcome and survive adversity and be strengthened by it. All it takes is a shift in thinking, a removal of the cloud that covers the brain of most mortals.

Life is a gift, no matter what the circumstances. What we do with that gift is up to us, for we create our own reality. There is an art to living. It's called being truly alive. You look and really see. You listen and really hear. You touch and really feel. You tune into the music of the winds, the music of the universe.

When you walk into a room and flip on a light, you illuminate the whole room. All the dark corners are removed. You can do the same thing with the spirit that is you. Allow the light that connects all that share this Mother Earth to illuminate the inner child and rekindle the flame of the real truths that surround us. All you must do is ask in a sincere and humble way, and all answers will be given. We are never alone.

Every breath you take is shared by all. Every moment is awash with something different and new. It will never be the same again. Every sunset is different. Every cloud formation constantly changes and evolves.

Peace

As the sun peaks over the mountaintop, it's the beginning of a new day.

I touch Mother Earth; I feel the warmth she gives me.

I look up to Father Sky and see the love he has for me.

I see an eagle fly and feel the grace and peace in him.

The cool breeze of the trees falls upon my face.

The raging river is like the heart of a great warrior.

As night falls, Grandmother Moon shines upon my face, and I know that Grandfather (the Great Spirit) is watching over me.

I can rest in Peace!

May the Great Spirit fill your days and nights with love, happiness, and Peace.

Written by Strong Spirit

Setting Up An Altar for Meditation

This section is devoted to setting up an inside altar, a place for sacred tools and objects, such as smudging feathers and crystals. This should be your sacred spot where no one enters or touches—your positive vibrational area where harmony and balance prevail. Remember, harmony is beauty in motion.

Walk around your dwelling and see what feels right to you—perhaps a small table under a window facing south or perhaps a quiet space that radiates the early morning dawn light from the east. Listen to the inner you. Let the true you be your guide.

I have a small table made of hickory and twigs, a twig table with a small lambskin rug in front to sit on. A candle representing the south is on top of my altar. The candle sits in a small circle of gopher dirt, which is on an abalone shell. The shell represents the west and water. The gopher dirt represents the north and Mother Earth. Any being (such as a mole or gopher) that dwells in and works Mother Earth is truly sacred.

A replica of my totem beings is present, and a feather is there for smudging and to represent the east and air. My table faces south, the direction of renewal and rebirth, the red road. A window allows light to illuminate the altar. My pipe (chanunpa) hangs in its carrier on the west wall of my bedroom. But what is right for me may not feel correct for you. What I say is simply a guideline—an arrow that points the way. Only you can find the pathway that is truly yours. By the way, never blow out your candle. Extinguish the flame with a utensil made for such. To use your breath is to show dishonor.

All is simplicity, for truth in life is simple. Only people try to complicate everything.

In the morning give thanks for the gift of life as you greet each new dawn. At night (or when you feel the need), visit your altar for a quiet moment. Be ready to serve, and be ready to receive. The gifts of knowledge will increase.

The conscious and unconscious mind requires purification, or negativity, and its accompanying fear will creep in. Then the whole system becomes unbalanced and negative. Always venture inward.

Spirit lessons can materialize in visions, dreams, and meditation. Remember that love is energy. Love yourself in an unselfish way, and love Mother Earth. Listen and really hear. Look and really see. Touch and really feel. All you will ever need to know is there for the asking. Be humble and sincere.

Before the word there was light—not emotion, but the energy of light, the root of truth. When you open the door to your heart and radiate light, you will walk in the pathway of truth. The inner you is a part of that eternal light. So listen with inner hearing to your inner sound. Always venture within to the light when you meditate. Then focus in a detached way so you can make proper choices (not emotional ones) or be directed by the spirit that is you. Truth will come. It will awaken you, and balance will occur; for balance and harmony are truth.

Don't hang onto ego, the unwanted, and the unnecessary emotions of the past or present. That would be ignorance at play. Wisdom is always present. The choice between really knowing and ignoring truth is up to you—wisdom over ignorance, health over disease, joy over sorrow. We can hold on or release—flow free or block. Every cell has all of this knowledge, a gift of love from the heart of the Great Spirit. What we do from here on out will influence greatly the magnitude of the earth changes now taking place. The life force of the planet— our Mother/Grandmother's survival—is at stake. We have all been like bad children, building sand castles, tearing each other's down, and starting over. Time as we see it is but an arrangement of energy patterns called events. Stress can cause your energy or vibration to become altered. What each of us feels affects the whole universe and galaxies beyond. Therefore, it is essential that we meditate and find solitude. Our body is an extension of who we are, and every cell is programmed to hear every thought you project. We are all a part of this universe. Love this planet.

Remember, love is energy. Love and respect all our brothers and sisters that share this space. I mean the winged, four-legged, trees (tall ones), plants, rocks, reptiles, water beings, insects. They are great teachers if we but listen. And don't judge other two-legged beings. They move at their own pace.

You must completely empty the glass before you pour in the light of truth. Otherwise, you will only have more muddied water, instead of a glass of pure water or truth. Silence is golden. You learn in silence.

Winter is a good time for healing, for shamanic journeys, for vision quests, as Eagle flies high.

To the Cherokee (my people), the cedar is sacred, stained by the blood of a mean-spirited sorcerer. Therefore, it is a Medicine Tree, used on ceremonial occasions, for smudge, sticks, stone, people lodges (sweat), etc. Its smoke drives away evil spirits and ghosts that wish to harm. It is of the sun and the element fire—the world tree, representing renewal and life.

Sweetgrass is also used as a purifier and in various ceremonies. Stomachaches, toothache, fever, purification, and cramps were/are treated with sweetgrass. It was once used as a medium of exchange because of its value.

The name *sage* comes from the Latin word *salvia* (healthy). Nervous disorders, wound healing, fever lowering, and indigestion brought on by fatty foods (such as sausage) are treated by sage. It acts as a calming agent. You may want to put a bit of sage, cedar, or sweetgrass on your altar or burn a bit in your flame. Sage is often tucked behind the ear to keep malevolent spirits from whispering to you during meditation or ceremonies.

Frankincense (representing spirituality) and myrrh (earth spirituality) were used by the early Christians, but I prefer cedar, which was also mentioned in the Bible.

Remember, meditate, contemplate, and radiate—Mother Earth needs your healing light, so keep shining.

Nansih Spirit Song and Companion

In nature, there is unity, variety, and life. Though each day ends in darkness, darkness then leads to a new day. Let nature in all its wisdom guide each new day of your life, and may you be blessed with living, learning, and light.

------*Nansih*

Visual Healing
of Animals

Start by calming the animal with light strokes. Make one and one-half inch circles all over the body, as well as stroking of the ears, paws, or feet if the animal does not object. This is known in part as the Tellington Touch.

Surround the animal and the work area with a white light to sterilize and create an electric magnetic field throughout—visual, of course. Use the rock and color of your choice.

Visualize a clean muslin cloth being pulled by you through the nose of the animal (white light) and through the body—sinus, neck, legs, body whole—pulling to convert to a higher level. See the cloth as being very, very clean. After you have done this, visualize the cloth being incinerated. Next, visualize the animal in a tub bath of blue healing energy, saturated in blue water, soaking, soaking, soaking. Then change the water color to pink. See it soaking into the tissues, bones, organs, head—a sterilizing light. Flash with a white light, then out of the tub into pure white linen representing the white Christ light. Blow indigo blue smoke into the body; then use a suctioning tube to remove any residue from the nostrils. Visualize pink in the ears. Close the suction hole with a visual laser beam.

Finish with a one-fourth inch white light, then blue, then white again. The white light around the animal seals like a round steel beam. It puts a white cosmic seal around the whole body. Take five-inch blue, then five-inch white again, then five-inch blue, and finish with the white seal, forming a hard seal against any disease.

If any organ is malfunctioning, work on that area in the same way as you would the whole body. Do the organ first, seal it, then work on the whole body.

Note: You may want to shake your hands loosely to remove any negative charge; then rub them together to produce positive energy before beginning the massage technique.

Final Thoughts

In rose-colored retrospect and quiet reflection, I have tried to float to paper, as feathers drifting earthward, adverbs, adjectives, and nouns, I hope in fairly lucid order. One tiny written word follows quietly behind another tiny written word until page after page is completed.

Miracles do still occur because it is a miracle this book was written at all. Sleep had to be sacrificed because daylight hours do not provide the quiet required for constructive thought processing. So, each night, for many a moon, while the refuge inhabitants slumbered, I would take pen in hand and work into the wee hours of pre-dawn.

André would curl by my side being ever so careful not to touch the writing pad as he kneaded his paws and purred—content to finally have his favorite person all to himself. His companionship became invaluable. He also kept me abreast of the time. Cessation of purring and ten to fifteen yawns in a row meant we must quit and allow mind and body to rest. My "big baby" black and white cat with the macho man swagger should be considered co-author. He certainly helped.

The sketch of yours truly was done by a Native American Indian who also happens to be a spiritual leader for the Cherokees in Texas. My thanks to Scott Sun Eagle.

Throughout my life, I have been privileged to know myriad good and intelligent people worldwide—people of all types of beliefs, from all walks of life who have graciously shared their accumulative knowledge with this seeker of new truths. Perhaps I gravitate toward individuals who possess intellect, or perhaps they gravitate toward souls of an inquisitive nature. Whatever the reason, I am thankful for their wisdom, their love, and their friendship. I could not have survived without that constant unending support. Life is not always easy, nor do I think it was meant to be. But my friends have made it easier. They are a blessing. They have also helped in the expansion of my horizons, and I hope in some small way this book will be a reminder to them that faith can indeed move mountains.

We think that when we become adults, we will have all the answers. Now there are some answers; but many more questions have evolved, and a hunger for knowledge to expand a memory bank of experience for future reference exists. There is a quest for truth and inner harmony. A desire to live life with questions and the adventure of nature, of reading, learning, and always the presence of laughter exists.

I ask that you join with me in learning to make choices for yourself, to explore new ideas, to consider new avenues not thought of before, to thirst for knowledge, to set aside fear of change, to search out the part of us all that desires to grow, to allow yourself to question, to feel alive, to be responsible for your life, and to take charge—to have insight, to use all the senses, to stir, to live, to tolerate, and to help.

Don't ever be afraid of what people may think. Only the ignorant and uneducated laugh at things not understood. They are the ones that fear change, so always be true to yourself and move forward. We are all exploring, developing, and growing. Our paths and the keenness of insight may be different. But this present life is not a dress rehearsal. It is the real production, so let's move ahead. Remember that wisdom and knowledge cut through delusion, and the greater power of the mind is imagination. It directs the reality of our todays and our futures. In so doing, it releases us from the hold and the mistakes of the past. Don't be locked in.

We all have a purpose for being here and a pathway to follow. I never expected to be a "maintainer" of a refuge. Childhood governesses, tutors, private and preparatory schools provided by a father who was a financial genius did much to provide me with a proper education—all background and knowledge for my present endeavors. But it didn't alter my pathway. I was born a naturalist and at an early age preferred the ethereal beauty of the Everglades and the sun-warmed sands of isolated inlets and beaches to any of the events offered by my circle of so-called jet setters in Florida.

We profit mentally and spiritually from every experience we are involved in, and I shall always be indebted to my parents for showing me many. They provided me with life. They provided the gene structuring that set into motion whatever talents I now possess, along with the ones that I brought into this life experience. When they were gone, my former guardians, Norma and Jimmy Keller of Miami Beach, continued the programming. I thank God for them all. I am grateful. They gave me roots, and they gave me wings.

My beautiful and gentle mother, Memiwah or Grace Evelyn, possessed wondrous reverence for the natural beauty of the world and for the spirit present in all living things. She instilled in me this respect for all that is God-created and a commitment to preserve and protect. She was wise in knowing that if cruelty and lack of respect for any living creature are taught to a child, he or she will then be cruel to his or her own peer group, to adults, to anything, as sociologists and psychologists have proven in their studies of civilizations, including ours.

This book, along with the one to follow, *Trees, the Everlasting Wisdom and Beauty,* is my small way of saying thanks.

I can remember my mother's black eyes flashing as she asked her precocious child the reason or purpose in always asking "Why? Why? Why?" about everything. I answered, "Why not?" and, so it goes . . .

May your spirit always find your own bluebonnet trails, and may you be blessed with

Sapphire skies, a circle of light
Golden moonbeams, a starlit night
Breathtaking rainbows, and swifts in flight.

Nansih

About the Author

Nansih Spirit Song honors and is proud of her Cherokee heritage.

As a child, her grandmother gave her the name of Spirit Song because Nan always said, "Everything has spirit and a song to sing." She still believes that.

Nansih maintains a wildlife refuge. At one time, she was a state/federal rehabber being bitten by creatures from alligators to eagles. She was one of the founders of the 200th chapter of the National Audubon Society, covering five counties. Nansih wrote a weekly column for five papers and published a monthly, then quarterly, newsletter that covered the globe. Nansih also did television programs in Palestine, Texas, and Lufkin, Texas, always advocating the care of the universe in her lectures as well. In the late 1980s she wrote a successful pet care book on using herbs and natural means for healing.

Born in the Smoky Mountains of East Tennessee (where she still maintains a redwood cabin), she was raised and educated in Miami Beach, Florida.

The Wolf clan is part of her heritage, and she had relatives in the long ago Longhair clan. The latter were considered healers. A loving grandmother and mother Memiwah began teaching Nansih at an early age. They gave her wings and a firm foundation. Their spirits live on.

The information contained in this booklet is not intended as a substitute for competent medical advice. All matters relating to personal health require qualified medical supervision.